AF599210

SINGER AND CULTURAL ICON

by Rachel Rose

Minneapolis, Minnesota

Credits

Cover and title page, © Jason LaVeris/Getty Images; 5, © Erika Goldring/Contributor/Getty Images; 6, © Curtis Hilbun/AFF-USA.COM/MEGA/Newscom/TALOS/Newscom; 7, © Michael Ochs Archives/Stringer/Getty Images; 8, © AevanStock/Shutterstock; 9, © Michael Ochs Archives/Stringer/Getty Images; 10, © defotoberg/Shutterstock; 11, © JDFree/Shutterstock; 12, © Jack Fordyce/Shutterstock; 13, © Archive Photos/Stringer/Getty Images; 14, © Ron Galella, Ltd./Contributor/Getty Images; 15, © Michael Gordon/Shutterstock; 16, © Gareth Davies/Contributor/Getty Images; 17, © Gareth Davies/Contributor/Getty Images; 19, © Kevin Winter/Staff/Getty Images; 20, © Carl Beust/Shutterstock; 21, © Kevin Winter/Staff/Getty Images

Bearport Publishing Company Product Development Team

President: Jen Jenson; Director of Product Development: Spencer Brinker; Senior Editor: Allison Juda; Editor: Charly Haley; Associate Editor: Naomi Reich; Senior Designer: Colin O'Dea; Associate Designer: Elena Klinkner; Associate Designer: Kayla Eggert; Product Development Assistant: Anita Stasson

Library of Congress Cataloging-in-Publication Data

Names: Rose, Rachel, 1968- author.
Title: Dolly Parton : singer and cultural icon / by Rachel Rose.
Description: Minneapolis, Minnesota : Bearport Publishing Company, 2023. | Series: Bearport biographies | Includes bibliographical references and index.
Identifiers: LCCN 2022036355 (print) | LCCN 2022036356 (ebook) | ISBN 9798885094023 (library binding) | ISBN 9798885095242 (paperback) | ISBN 9798885096393 (ebook)
Subjects: LCSH: Parton, Dolly--Juvenile literature. | Country musicians--United States--Biography--Juvenile literature. | Singers--United States--Biography--Juvenile literature.
Classification: LCC ML3930.P25 H65 2022 (print) | LCC ML3930.P25 (ebook) | DDC 782.421642092 [B]--dc23/eng/20220729
LC record available at https://lccn.loc.gov/2022036355
LC ebook record available at https://lccn.loc.gov/2022036356

For more information, write to Bearport Publishing, 5357 Penn Avenue South, Minneapolis, MN 55419.

Contents

A Lifetime of Good

Dolly Parton made her way to the stage. With her **iconic** big hair and bright, glittery outfit, all eyes were on her. The crowd jumped to their feet to clap and cheer.

Dolly was about to accept the Willie Nelson Lifetime Achievement **Award**. It honored her long music **career** and **humanitarian** work.

Dolly has been writing and singing hit songs for more than 60 years!

Dolly received her lifetime achievement award in 2016.

An Early Start

Dolly was born on January 19, 1946, in Locust Ridge, Tennessee. She was part of a big family with 12 children. They all lived together in a small, one-bedroom cabin. Her whole family shared a love of music. Dolly started writing songs when she was five. When she was eight, Dolly got her first guitar from her uncle Bill.

Dolly with her uncle Bill Owens

When she was 10, Dolly started **performing** on local television and radio shows.

Big Dreams

As soon as Dolly finished high school, she followed her dreams to become a music star. She moved to Nashville, Tennessee, and her uncle helped her meet other musicians. In 1967, she teamed up with country singer Porter Wagoner. The two had several hit songs together. Then, Dolly went solo in 1974.

Nashville is also known as Music City.

Dolly met her husband, Carl Dean, on her first day in Nashville. Her popular song "Jolene" was about a woman who had flirted with him.

Dolly worked with Porter Wagoner *(left)* for seven years.

People loved Dolly's songs. Many of Dolly's hits, the singer wrote herself. She used music to tell stories about her life. One of her favorite songs, "Coat of Many Colors," is a story about a coat her mother made for her when she was little. Even though she was teased about how it looked, Dolly loved her coat.

Dolly has written more than 3,000 songs and recorded more than 450 of them.

WARNER
WARNER BROS.

All-Around Star

Soon, Dolly became known for more than just her singing and songwriting. She stood out on the movie screen, too.

The **cultural** icon used her growing fame to **explore** other talents. In 1980, she starred in the movie *9 to 5*. Since then, she has been in more than 20 movies.

Dolly likes to wear sparkly and colorful outfits.

Dolly is known for her big hair. She says she owns at least 365 wigs—one for every day of the year!

Dolly *(left)* with her costars from *9 to 5*

Dolly became a successful businesswoman, too! In 1986, Dolly opened the Dollywood theme park near where she grew up in Tennessee. Today, about three million people visit the park every year.

Dolly has many other businesses, including a record company called Dolly Records. As of now, she is the only singer to make music for the company.

Dolly often feels sick on rides. The only ride she goes on at Dollywood is the Ferris wheel.

SHOWSTREET
PALACE THEATER
Dollywood

Giving Back

With all her success, Dolly wanted to give back to her childhood community. It was very important to her that kids have a good education. In 1995, she started a program in Tennessee that sends free books to young children. For the older kids near her Locust Ridge childhood home, Dolly started to help students pay for **college**.

Dolly's book giveaway is called Dolly Parton's Imagination Library.

Dolly became known as the Book Lady in the area where she grew up.

Over the years, Dolly's book program has grown. Now, she sends millions of books to children around the world. She raises money for other worldwide causes, too. Dolly cares about animal rights and helping people during **natural disasters**. In 2020, Dolly gave a lot of money to help the fight against COVID-19.

Dolly gives about $1 million to **charities** every year.

Dolly performs at events that help raise money for different causes.

Going Strong

Dolly has had a lot of success in her life. She has wowed fans on the stage and on the big screen. All the while, she has continued to give back through all of her charity work. And Dolly Parton fans will be happy to hear she shows no signs of stopping!

In November 2022, Dolly was added to the Rock & Roll Hall of Fame.

Timeline

Here are some key dates in Dolly Parton's life.

Born on January 19

Moves to Nashville

1967

Teams up with Porter Wagoner

1974

Starts her solo career

1986

Opens Dollywood

1995

Starts her book program

Receives Willie Nelson Lifetime Achievement Award

2022

Joins the Rock & Roll Hall of Fame

Glossary

award a prize for being the best at something

career a lifelong job

charities groups that try to help people in need

college a school where people go to learn after high school

cultural the customs, ideas, art, and way of life for a group of people

explore to search in order to discover something new

humanitarian a person who works to improve the lives of other people

iconic well-known

natural disasters events caused by nature that result in great loss, hardship, and damage

performing entertaining an audience

Index

Read More

Felix, Rebecca. *Dolly Parton (Checkerboard Biographies)*. Minneapolis: Abdo Publishing, 2022.

Moening, Kate. *Dolly Parton: Country Music Star (Women Leading the Way)*. Minneapolis: Bellwether Media, 2021.

Learn More Online

1. Go to **www.factsurfer.com** or scan the QR code below.
2. Enter "**Dolly Parton**" into the search box.
3. Click on the cover of this book to see a list of websites.

About the Author

Rachel Rose is a writer who lives in San Francisco. Her favorite books to write are about people who lead inspiring lives.